Cooking in World Cultures

Food and Cooking in
Ancient Egypt

Written by Clive Gifford
Illustrations by Paul Cherrill

PowerKiDS
press
New York

Published in 2010 by The Rosen Publishing Group Inc.
29 East 21st Street, New York, NY 10010

First Edition

Series Editor: Victoria Brooker
Editor: Susie Brooks
Designer: Jason Billin
Picture researcher: Shelley Noronha
Food consultant: Stella Sargeson

Library of Congress Cataloging-in-Publication Data

Gifford, Clive.
  Food and cooking in ancient Egypt / Clive Gifford.
       p. cm. -- (Cooking in world cultures)
  Includes index.
  ISBN 978-1-61532-337-1 (library binding)
  ISBN 978-1-61532-359-3 (paperback)
  ISBN 978-1-61532-360-9 (6-pack)
  1. Diet--Egypt--History--Juvenile literature. 2. Cookery, Egyptian--History--
Juvenile literature. 3. Food habits--Egypt--History--Juvenile literature. I. Title.
  TX360.E3G54 2010
  394.1'20932--dc22

                              2009024058

Photographs:
3, 24 akg-images/Electa; 5 © Gemma Ivern/istock.com; 6 Luke
Daniek/istock.com; 7 Werner Forman Archive/ British Museum,
London; 8 The Art Archive/Gianni Dagli Orti; 9 akg-images/James
Morris; 10 Werner Forman Archive/The Louvre, Paris; 12 The Art
Archive/Pharaonic Village Cairo/Gianni Dagli Orti; cover, 13, 16,
18, 22 akg-images /Erich Lessing; 14 The Art Archive/Archaeological
Museum Florence/Gianni Dagli Orti; 15 Werner Forman Archive/
E. Strouhal; 20 Tibor Bognar/Corbis; 23 The Art Archive/Ragab Papyrus
Institute Cairo/ Gianni Dagli Orti; 25 akg-images/Andrea Jemolo;
26 The Art Archive/Luxor Museum, Egypt/Gianni Dagli Orti;
28 The Art Archive/Egyptian Museum Turin/Gianni Dagli Orti;
29 akg-images/François Guenet

Manufactured in China

CPSIA Compliance Information: Batch #WAW0102PK: For Further Information

contact Rosen Publishing, New York, New York at 1-800-237-9932

Contents

An amazing civilization

More than 5,000 years ago, the ancient Egyptians created an amazing **civilization**—one of the oldest and longest-running in the world. They transformed their North African homeland into a center of farming, building, and invention that thrived for over 3,000 years.

Ahead of their time

The ancient Egyptians made enormous advances in science, technology, and medicine. They also developed an organized system of government, led for many centuries by a powerful ruler. They built large cities, giant temples, and incredible funeral **pyramids** for some of their rulers. The Great Pyramid at Giza, built around 2570 BCE, stood as the world's biggest single building for more than 3,800 years!

Cooking clues

The ancient Egyptians left behind few recipes and no cookbooks. However, people who study ancient Egyptian history, often called Egyptologists, have done lots of detective work. They have found many clues about the foods and ingredients that were used all those years ago—and how they were farmed, prepared, and cooked.

► *This map shows the Nile and some of the most important settlements in Ancient Egypt.*

4

Ancient treasures

Archaeologists have unearthed a huge number of exciting **artefacts** from ancient Egypt. Many were discovered in tombs, where wealthy ancient Egyptians were buried with some of their belongings. The burial tomb of the couple Kha and Merit, for example, was found in 1906. Among the items inside was a small metal cauldron that was used to cook porridge.

The ancient Egyptians also produced lots of written records and painted or carved scenes of everyday life. All these treasures help to give people today an idea of how the rich and poor lived, worked, ate, and drank.

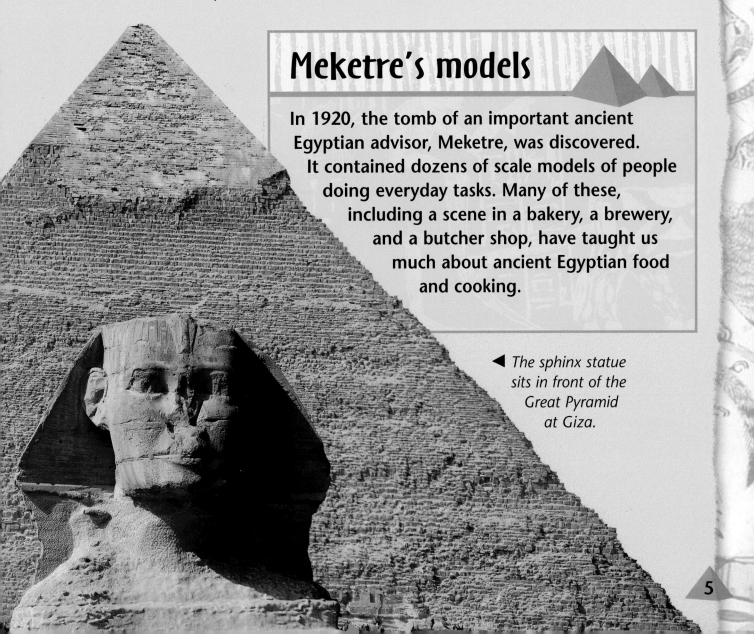

Meketre's models

In 1920, the tomb of an important ancient Egyptian advisor, Meketre, was discovered. It contained dozens of scale models of people doing everyday tasks. Many of these, including a scene in a bakery, a brewery, and a butcher shop, have taught us much about ancient Egyptian food and cooking.

◄ *The sphinx statue sits in front of the Great Pyramid at Giza.*

Fruits of the Nile

Ancient Egypt was dominated by the great River Nile, which runs for more than 4,100 miles (6,600 kilometers) through several African countries. The Nile was the main transportation link between northern and southern Egypt. Traders carrying goods sailed up and down its length.

River of life

Egypt's climate is hot and dry with little rain. The Nile provided the ancient Egyptians with fresh water to drink and **irrigate** their fields. The only land suitable for crops lay in a relatively narrow strip on either side of the river. This was where most ancient Egyptians lived.

Every year, usually starting in June, the Nile flooded its banks. Farmers channeled the overflowing water along canals and trapped it in ponds and small lakes to be used later. The flood was also a great benefit to the soil. When the waters receded, they left behind thick layers of mud, sand, and silt. These were full of **nutrients** that helped to make the soil more **fertile**.

▼ Farmland beside the banks of the river Nile. For thousands of years, the Nile has been crucial to food production in Egypt.

Fish and birds

The ancient Egyptians caught many species of fish from the Nile, including mullet, carp, catfish, perch, and bolti. They fished with a simple rod and hook, or large nets stretched out between two boats.

The Nile was also home to a wide variety of birds. Ducks and wild geese were the most common, living mainly in the reedy marshes close to the river's banks. There were herons, pelicans, and cranes, too. The ancient Egyptians hunted birds for food. Sometimes they used cats to flush them out of the reeds. On other occasions, they trapped birds by throwing out large nets with weights in the corners.

▲ *An ancient Egyptian hunts birds on the river. He stands on a small boat made of bundles of reeds.*

Useful shadouf

The shadouf is one of the oldest water-moving devices in the world. It is made up of a long pole with a bucket on a rope at one end and a weight, such as a large rock, at the other. The bucket can be lowered into water, then raised up with ease by using the weighted pole like a lever.

Farming the fields

Most ordinary Egyptians, unless they had a trade such as making pottery, were farmers. Some worked their own small fields, but others were employed by wealthy landowners.

Meat and dairy

Farmers needed the best soil for growing crops, so there was little grassy pasture for grazing **livestock**. Cattle and goats were kept mainly for their milk, and occasionally for their meat, too. Some people reared and ate pigs, even though they were sacred to the god Seth. They also tried farming hyenas, but this soon stopped—probably because the animals were fierce and the meat was tough to eat.

Ordinary ancient Egyptians ate much less meat than wealthy nobles and **merchants**. Many families had chickens or geese, which provided them with eggs. The milk they got from goats and cows turned sour quickly in the hot climate. Most of it was made into cheese.

◀ A farmer uses cattle to help plow his field.

Floods and fights

A farmer's work was set out by the seasons and by the rise and fall of the river Nile.

When the floods came, they often caused disputes by washing away the boundaries between different farmers' fields. Teams of officials, called rope-stretchers, would re-measure the fields using a rope 12 **cubits** (about 6.5 yards or 6 meters) in length.

▲ *This wall painting shows fields being measured after a flood.*

Colorful crops

Planting began shortly after the floods disappeared, in October or November. The land was prepared using wooden plows with blades of wood, bronze, or **flint**. Farmers scattered the seed by hand, then drove animals over the field to tread it in. Soon, the land became a patchwork of crops including wheat, barley, many types of peas and beans, and other vegetables, such as lettuces, onions, radishes, and cucumbers.

As the crops grew, there was much work to be done. Fields had to be weeded, watered, and protected from birds and wild animals. Harvest time, usually in March or April, was the most important time of year. People prayed and made offerings to the gods for a good, abundant harvest.

Ancient Egyptian beer

The ancient Egyptians liked brewing beer. Often, they used loaves of barley bread, crumbled and mixed with toasted grains and water. The end result was thick and lumpy, but filling. Children drank it as well as adults—at breakfast, lunch, and dinner! **Inscriptions** found at the pyramids of Giza show that the workmen there were given beer three times a day.

Food for the day

Most ancient Egyptians ate three meals, with evening dinner being the main meal. Breakfast was often hot and filling. It gave people energy for a long day of hard physical work in the fields or working on building projects.

Lunchtime snack

Lunch for many ancient Egyptians was simple and quick. Workers usually took a packed lunch of bread and beer, sometimes with a vegetable, such as a leek, cucumber, or onion, on the side.

It's rotten!

For most of the year, the weather was hot. This meant that food spoiled quickly. The ancient Egyptians had no refrigerators and ice was unknown, so they learned other ways of preserving food, such as salting and sun-drying.

▲ *This stone relief shows Princess Nefertiabt sitting down at a table with offerings of food.*

Preserving food

Salt was plentiful in some parts of Egypt and acted as a preservative. Luxuries such as fish, chicken, and some meats were covered in salt or pickled in salty water. Many common foods, including beans, chickpeas, and some vegetables, were dried in the sun for later use.

Ful medames

Ful medames was a popular breakfast dish in Ancient Egypt.
It is still eaten by Egyptians today.

Serves 4

You will need:

2 x 16 oz. (450g) cans broad
  beans in water
1–2 garlic cloves, crushed
1 tablespoon lemon juice

1½ tablespoons olive oil
½ teaspoon cumin
⅜ cup (100ml) of water
Knob of butter
4 eggs
4 pita breads

1. Drain and rinse the broad beans.

2. Put the beans in a bowl, with
   the garlic, lemon juice, olive
   oil, cumin, and water, and
   mash together roughly.

3. Put the mixture in the pan and heat slowly for
   4–5 minutes, stirring occasionally.

4. Meanwhile, melt the butter in a pan
   to fry the eggs and warm your pita bread
   in an oven or toaster.

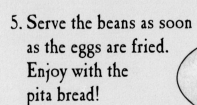

5. Serve the beans as soon
   as the eggs are fried.
   Enjoy with the
   pita bread!

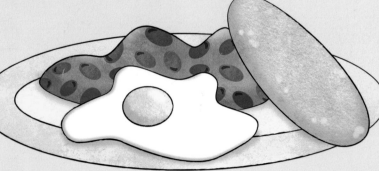

Egyptian kitchens

Ancient Egyptian kitchens were usually very simple. Most were outdoors, either in a courtyard or on the flat terraced roof of a home. Sometimes, a lightly thatched roof was built over the kitchen. This gave shade while allowing smoke from the cooking to escape.

Cooks

Women were in charge of cooking. They usually prepared food sitting down, on reed mats or at low tables. Young children would often help. Pottery jars, sacks, and small drawstring bags made from leather were used to store ingredients.

Cooking tools

Most households used a variety of kitchen tools, including whisks for beating liquids, ladles, spoons, and spatulas. **Archaeologists** have also found examples of sieves and strainers, woven from dried-out reeds. Kitchen knives were made with copper or bronze blades—or a sharp piece of **flint** if you were poor.

▼ *This ancient Egyptian noble's kitchen has a cone-shaped clay oven and a shelf of pottery storage jars.*

Ancient ovens

People used simple pans and trays to bake with. They heated water and soups in large clay pots with two handles. Boiling, braising, and other forms of cooking were done on an open fire, in a hearth made of stone or clay. Sometimes a **brazier,** a little bit like a large, round barbecue, was used.

Domed-shaped ovens made of clay were common, too. Underneath was a burning fire, with the airflow controlled by a small hatch to one side. Cooks roasted or baked many foods in these ovens, using long sticks to push items in and to pull them out.

▲ *An Egyptian woman pulls out flat breads from a clay oven.*

Fire starter

Many kitchen fires were lit using a device called a bow drill. This involved twisting a rod in a hole to create lots of heat through friction. The heat would set fire to some straw. Twigs, leaves, and even animal dung were then added to the flames. People tried not to burn too much wood or **charcoal,** because these were in limited supply. A large **papyrus** or palm leaf was used to fan the fire to keep it going.

Bread

No food was more important to the ancient Egyptians than bread. It was part of almost every meal. Barley and different forms of wheat, which are used to make bread, were ancient Egypt's biggest crops.

Grappling with grain

Turning crops to flour in ancient times was incredibly hard work. After the wheat or barley was harvested, it was trampled on by cattle. This helped to separate the ears of the crop, which contained the grain, from the straw stalks below. Next, the grain inside the ears had to be split from its outer covering, called the chaff. This was done by tossing basketfuls into the air, over and over again. The breeze would carry away the light chaff, while the heavier grain stayed in the basket.

At the grindstone

It was a woman's job to grind grain into flour between two large, flat stones. This was back-breaking work. Producing enough flour for a day's baking in one household could take several hours.

▶ *A woman grinds grain between the stone she holds and a large stone on the floor.*

Basic bread

The most common type of bread in ancient Egypt was made with just flour and water. Cooks kneaded and pressed it into flat, pancakelike shapes. These were baked on a shelf or grill above an open fire, or on the side of a hot clay oven. The end result was a little like the pita bread you can buy today.

Fancy loaves

Flat bread was not the Egyptians' only recipe. Some breads were flavored with honey, oil, or fruits such as figs. Others were savory, with sesame seeds and strong spices. Sometimes, clay molds were used to make breads in unusual cone- or bird-shapes. Experts believe there were more than 30 different types of bread in ancient Egypt.

Worn-out teeth

During the grain-grinding process, bits of sand and stone often got into the flour. This meant that most Egyptian bread was very coarse and gritty. It scraped people's teeth like sandpaper, meal after meal, day after day. **Archaeologists** have found many skeletons with teeth worn down to stumps.

◀ *An ancient Egyptian bakery at work. The two men standing at the table are kneading the bread dough.*

Fruit and vegetables

Most ancient Egyptians ate some fruit, but vegetables were a much bigger part of their diet. Peas and beans were particularly popular.

Scrumptious salads

The fields around the Nile were full of salad vegetables such as cucumbers, lettuces, onions, endives, and raphanus (a type of wild radish that tasted like a turnip). Egyptian lettuces were taller than today's. People ate the leaves whole, usually dipped in oil and salt. They also munched on whole, raw onions, just as we'd eat an apple!

Write and bite

The **papyrus** plant had a double use. Its fibers were made into paperlike scrolls for Egyptian **scribes** to write and draw on. Young papyrus shoots were also edible. They were soft and tender, similar to the bamboo shoots that people cook with today.

Fig-picking baboons

The fig was one of the most highly-prized Egyptian fruits. Egyptologists believe that some ancient Egyptians even trained baboons to climb trees and collect the figs for them!

▶ Farmers collect figs with the help of trained baboons.

16

Stuffed cabbage leaves

The ancient Egyptians considered cabbages to be one of the most tasty vegetables. This recipe is based on some of the ingredients they would have used.

Serves 4 as a snack

You will need:

1 savoy cabbage
1 onion, finely chopped
1 teaspoon sesame seeds
⅓ cup (50g) raisins
1 garlic clove, crushed

1 tablespoon of sesame oil
5 oz. (150g) fresh spinach, roughly chopped
½ teaspoon ground coriander
1¼ cup (300ml) vegetable stock
10 cocktail sticks

1. Carefully pick 12 soft leaves from inside the cabbage and cut off the stalk. Cook the leaves in boiling water for 2 minutes and then drain. Set aside to cool.

2. Fry the onion, sesame seeds, raisins, and garlic in the sesame oil for 2 minutes. Add the spinach and coriander, and cook for about 5 minutes, until everything is soft.

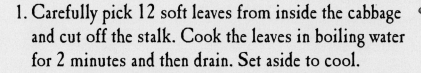

3. Divide the spinach mixture into 8–10 portions and place a portion on each cabbage leaf. Keep a couple of leaves spare in case you break one in the next step.

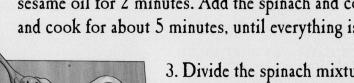

4. Roll each leaf around its filling, tucking in the sides to make a parcel. Secure with a cocktail stick.

5. Gently heat the stock in a large pan until it boils. Drop in the cabbage parcels, cover, and simmer over low heat for 5 minutes.

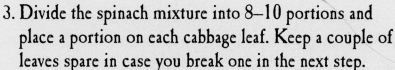
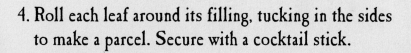

6. Remove the parcels with a slotted spoon. Take out the cocktail sticks and serve at once.

Sweet foods

The ancient Egyptians had no access to sugar but they still liked sweet foods. They used fruits, and occasionally honey, to create sweet dishes.

Fruity favorites

From paintings and archaeological finds, we know that the ancient Egyptians grew certain sweet fruits such as dates, figs, and grapes. These were sometimes eaten fresh, or dried in the sun and kept for when food was short. Grapes were also pressed and their juice made into a sweet, sticky syrup.

▲ Two Ancient Egyptians pick dates. Dates are rich in sugar and were sometimes used to make wine and syrups.

Sweet treats

Honey was known about in ancient Egypt but was very expensive. Unless you were a **pharaoh** or a noble in the pharaoh's service, it was a rare treat. An alternative sweetener was the root of the knotgrass plant. The Egyptians called this chuba and it grew throughout the Nile **delta**.

Healing honey

The Edwin Smith **Papyrus**, a scroll from the seventeenth century BCE, described how the ancient Egyptians used honey in medicine. They placed it on open wounds to help stop infection and to speed up the healing process. Honey contains small amounts of hydrogen peroxide (H_2O_2), a substance used today to fight infection.

Date Balls

This recipe uses both dates and honey to create a delicacy fit for a wealthy Egyptian noble. This rare recipe dates from around 1600 BCE and was discovered on a piece of ostraca, a shard of pottery used for writing by **scribes**.

You will need:

3 tablespoons honey
1⅓ cup (200g) fresh dates
1 teaspoon cinnamon

1¼ cup (100g) ground walnuts
A small bowl of ground almonds

Makes about 22 balls

1. Pour the honey into a small pan. On low heat, warm the honey without letting it boil. Remove from the heat.

2. Crush the dates with your hands or a spoon, and add some water to make a really thick paste.

3. Add the cinnamon and walnuts and mix.

4. Form small balls from the mixture about 1 inch (2.5cm) in diameter.

5. Coat each ball in the warm honey and roll in the dish of almonds to cover. Serve immediately.

Spice is nice

Compared to the vast range of sauces and spices we use today, the ancient Egyptians had only a handful of ways to add flavor to their food. These, though, were used heavily in their cooking.

Fiery flavors

The Egyptians loved strong flavors. They used a lot of garlic as well as spices such as aniseed, cumin, and cardamon. In later centuries, they discovered black pepper. These powerful flavors would sometimes mask the unpleasant taste of meat that was no longer fresh.

Seasoning

Cooking often involved herbs, including thyme, oregano, and mint. Salt was the most popular seasoning. People made their own oils by pressing linseed, sesame seeds, and the seeds of bushes, and trees, such as the Egyptian balsam tree. Fats from slaughtered animals were also used for cooking.

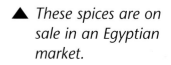

▲ *These spices are on sale in an Egyptian market.*

Weighty matters

Around 3500 BCE, the ancient Egyptians invented the first scales. They were used to weigh precious metals, and later, valuable spices. The scales consisted of two small pans hung on either end of a beam or pole. A spice was placed in one pan and balanced against a set of weights in the other.

Dukkah dip

Full of flavor, dukkah is a mixture of seeds, nuts, herbs, and spices. It was either sprinkled over meat or fish, or used like a dry dip as suggested here.

You will need:

⅔ cup (100g) sesame seeds
⅓ cup (50g) hazelnuts
½ cup (100g) blanched almonds
⅜ cup (50g) coriander seeds
2 tablespoons (15g) cumin seeds

¾ teaspoon salt
1 teaspoon dried thyme
Black pepper
1 flat bread, such as pita, per person
A small saucer of olive oil

Serves 4 as an appetizer or snack

1. Preheat your oven to 350°F (180°C). Place the sesame seeds on a baking sheet and the hazelnuts and almonds on another. When the oven is warm, cook the sesame seeds for 3 minutes and the nuts for 4 minutes.

2. Gently heat a heavy pan or skillet and toast the coriander and cumin seeds for about 3 minutes. Don't let them burn.

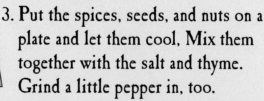

3. Put the spices, seeds, and nuts on a plate and let them cool, Mix them together with the salt and thyme. Grind a little pepper in, too.

4. Use either a pestle and mortar or a food processor to coarsely grind the mixture. Tip it into a bowl.

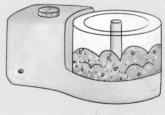

5. Eat by dipping some warmed flat bread into the olive oil and then dipping it into the dukkah.

Luxuries from abroad

By sailing down the River Nile and out into the Mediterranean Sea, the ancient Egyptians made contact with other lands and **civilizations**. They traded goods and brought some new foods and ingredients back home.

Goods to spare

In good harvest years, ancient Egypt often had surpluses of cereal crops, such as wheat and barley, to spare. Traders sold these far and wide, along with **papyrus**, linen, and some metals. Ancient Egyptian ships sailed the Mediterranean, Aegean, and Red Seas, and in the East, traders crossed land with groups of animals. Sometimes, they traveled through the harsh Sinai desert to Palestine and Syria to meet other traders. This is probably how spices such as cinnamon, originally grown in China, reached ancient Egypt.

Trading places

The ancient Egyptians sometimes fought wars with the Nubian people to the south of Egypt. But they also traded, bringing cattle, spices, ostrich eggs, and some types of wine back north. From the Middle Eastern region that we now call Lebanon came trees, cedar wood, and some nuts, especially walnuts and almonds.

▼ *Two workers load a boat with sacks of wheat before sailing on a trading journey.*

Rich and rare

Pomegranates and apples were imported from Palestine but were probably eaten only in small amounts by the rich and powerful. The pomegranates' seeds could be crushed and used as a flavoring. A dried pomegranate was found in the tomb of Djehuty, one of Queen Hatshepsut's officials.

As the centuries went by, the ancient Egyptians dealt more and more with other civilizations, including the ancient Greeks. Fruits such as quinces, pears, plums, and peaches were introduced, as well as pine nuts and pistachios.

▲ *This image, painted on papyrus, shows workers loading and unloading a large trading ship.*

The Land of Punt

Queen Hatshepsut became ruler of ancient Egypt around 3,500 years ago. During her reign, a mighty trading expedition was sent south to the mysterious Land of Punt. The expedition returned with many clay jars of incense and spices, myrrh trees, and wild animals, which probably included giraffes and lions. No one is sure exactly where Punt was, but it is thought to have been somewhere on the African east coast.

Gods and festivals

The ancient Egyptians worshiped many different gods. Some of these changed in importance over the centuries. For example, Amun was originally a minor god of wind, but centuries later, he became Amun-Re, the most powerful god of all. People celebrated the gods in processions and ceremonies known as festivals.

Everyday worship

Some gods were connected with people's jobs, such as Ptah who looked after craftspeople, and Thoth, the god of **scribes** and writing. The major gods had temples built for them, but people worshiped other gods in their homes. Taweret, the goddess of pregnant women, was one of these. Another was Bes, a dwarf god who was believed to keep evil spirits away. Bes's shape was often carved on beds and other furniture.

Impressive parades

The ancient Egyptians held many festivals, most of which honored a particular god. Their dates were often carved in stone calendars at temples. During major festivals, ordinary people stopped work and watched or took part in parades. Temple priests carried sacred statues of gods in processions that were watched by thousands.

▶ *A carved wooden sculpture of the god Taweret. It has the head and body of a hippopotamus.*

Festival foods

Rulers and local nobles often made generous food offerings at festival time. **Archaeologists** have discovered complete lists of festival foods, including numbers of geese, cattle, and the amount of grain needed for bread and beer. A lot of the food was shared between festivalgoers. It was a rare opportunity for ordinary ancient Egyptians to taste luxury goods such as wine and roasted beef.

Celebrating the reign

Although most festivals were religious, some were about celebrating a ruler's reign. Rameses III created a festival to mark his victory in battle over the Meshwesh (people from present-day Libya). Another important nonreligious festival was Heb-Sed, which honored any ruler who had been in power for 30 years.

▲ *The pharaoh Thutmose III (pictured left) makes an offering to the god Amun.*

Honoring Min

Min was a god connected to farming and fertility. At the festival to Min, held at the start of the harvest season, the ruler of ancient Egypt often cut the first **sheaf** of wheat or barley. Farmers offered Min food, such as small triangular loaves of bread, and prayed for a good harvest.

Feasts for the wealthy

Feasts were something that only wealthy Egyptians could afford. In their huge homes and palaces, they had storehouses, bakeries, and large kitchens. Dozens of servants worked long hours to prepare food for the feast menu.

▲ *This stone carving shows troupes of dancers, acrobats, and jugglers entertained at feasts, while musicians played instruments such as harps and lyres.*

Dressing up

Guests dressed up in their best clothes and jewelry for a feast. They covered themselves in perfumed lotions and many wore makeup, wigs, and lotus flowers. Often, guests would bring along their pets, including cats, dogs, and monkeys. During some feasts, a cone of perfumed wax was placed on the guests' heads. It slowly melted to give off a lovely scent.

Magnificent menu

A feast menu was made up of many different dishes. Roasted meats such as beef, antelope, and gazelle might have been served along with other delicacies, such as quails, pigeons and pelicans, cakes sweetened with honey, and fruits including figs. Some birds, such as cranes and geese, were force-fed in advance to fatten them up.

Fingers first

Feast guests sat on low benches or couches around the room. They ate with their fingers and drank wine and beer from goblets. Toward the end of the meal, servants would bring a bowl of scented water so that people could wash their hands.

Tasty chicken kebabs

These spicy chicken skewers make a great party snack. You could serve them with vegetables and rice or pita bread—or combine them with other recipes in this book and have a feast!

You will need:

⅜ cup (100ml) olive oil
1 onion, grated
3 garlic cloves, finely crushed
2 tablespoons ground cumin

1 teaspoon mild chili powder or paprika
14 oz. (400g) boneless chicken, cut into
 1 in. (2.5cm) cubes
1 small pot of plain yogurt
Small metal skewers   Serves 2

1. Mix together the oil, onion, garlic, and all the spices. This mixture is called the marinade. Pour into a large ziplock freezer bag and add the chicken.

2. Shake the bag carefully so that all the chicken is coated, then leave in a refrigerator for 4–6 hours.

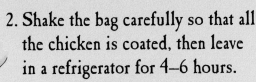

3. Remove the chicken from the bag and thread it onto the skewers. Pour the marinade into a dish.

4. Ask an adult to cook the chicken on a barbecue or under a broiler with a tray underneath. Turn the skewers and coat them regularly with marinade so that the chicken doesn't dry out.

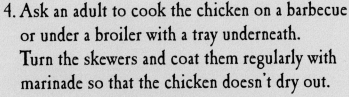

5. After 15–20 minutes, check that the chicken is cooked all the way through. Serve with a spoonful of yogurt on the side.

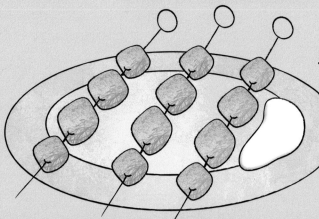

Food for the afterlife

The ancient Egyptians believed strongly in an afterlife—the idea of life after death. They believed that a person's spirit went on a long, difficult journey into the underworld, looking for the place where it would be judged by the gods.

Preparing the dead

The journey to the afterlife was so important to ancient Egyptians that they prepared the dead person's body very carefully. First, the brain and other organs were removed. Then the body was dried and wrapped in yards of linen cloth, coated with salts and resin. A ceremony, called the opening of the mouth, was performed by priests, who touched the mouth and eyes of the dead person. This was to enable the spirit to see, eat, and drink along its journey.

Funeral food

Many wealthy ancient Egyptians were buried in chambers called tombs. Food was usually buried with them, to nourish them on their way to the afterlife. An ox or large gazelle was often slaughtered at a funeral. Its heart, thought to be the most delicious and sacred part, was placed in the tomb along with some other prime cuts of meat. The rest of the animal was cooked and fed to the funeralgoers.

▼ *These breads were found in the funeral tomb of an Ancient Egyptian.*

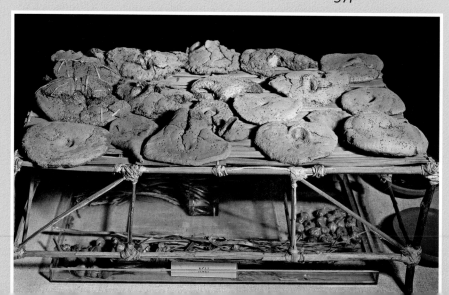

Endless offerings

Relatives continued to make offerings and prayers for many months and years after the funeral, at regular festivals for the dead. **Archaeologists** have discovered many foods in ancient Egyptian tombs, from dried fish and portions of duck, to wine jars and triangular bread loaves.

▲ *A collection of offerings to the dead are shown at a temple built for Queen Hatshepsut.*

Servants forever

In early ancient Egypt, the servants of some kings were killed and buried with their masters when they died. In later times, small models called shabtis or shawabtis were buried instead. Many of these were small wood or limestone carvings of kitchen servants baking bread or cooking meat. They were designed to serve the dead person in the afterlife.

King Tut's tomb

In 1922, the tomb of a young ancient Egyptian ruler called Tutankhamun was discovered. Among its many rich treasures were bread, fruit, clay jars of beer, 36 wine jars, and 413 shabti figures. In 2007, further finds in the tomb included eight baskets of a type of fruit called doum.

Glossary

archaeologist a person who studies human life in the past by finding and examining ancient items.

artefact an object from human history which has been recovered and may be studied to learn more.

brazier a type of container that holds a fire used for certain forms of cooking.

charcoal a black substance made from burned wood that can be used as a fuel

civilization a highly developed and organized society of people.

cubit a unit of measurement that roughly equals the length of an adult forearm or around 20 in. (50cm).

delta the area of land where the Nile river spreads out as it reaches the Mediterranean Sea.

fertile when used about land, it means that the soil and conditions are good for growing crops.

flint a hard form of quartz that is sometimes found with sharp edges. It was used as a simple tool.

inscription a short message carved or written onto an object.

irrigate to supply an area of land with water, particularly to allow crops to grow well.

livestock animals kept on a farm or elsewhere by people to eat, for the eggs, milk, or wool they produce or to sell at a market to make money.

merchant someone who buys and sells goods.

nutrients substances that help a living thing live, grow, and stay healthy.

papyrus a reedlike plant that the ancient Egyptians used to make sheets for writing on similar to paper.

pharaoh name used to describe a king or queen who ruled ancient Egypt.

pyramids large structures, usually with four sides. Many pyramids were built to house the bodies of pharaohs after their deaths.

scribe an official in ancient Egypt whose job was to write and to read.

sheaf a group or bundle of stalks of a cereal crop, such as wheat, which are cut from the plant.

Further Information and Web Sites

Books

History Beneath Your Feet: Ancient Egypt by Jane Shuter (Raintree, 1999)

Rich and Poor in Ancient Egypt by Clare Hibbert (Smart Apple Media, 2005)

The Egyptians: Life in Ancient Egypt by Liz Sonneborn (Millbrook Press, 2009)

Web Sites

Due to the changing nature of Internet links, PowerKids Press has developed an online list of Web sites related to the subject of this book. This site is updated regularly. Please use this link to access this list:
http://www.powerkidslinks.com/ciwc/egypt/

Index